COCHISE

APACHE CHIEF

LARISSA PHILLIPS

rosen central
Primary Source™
The Rosen Publishing Group, Inc., New York

Published in 2004 by The Rosen Publishing Group, Inc.
29 East 21st Street, New York, NY 10010

Copyright © 2004 by The Rosen Publishing Group, Inc.

First Edition

Library of Congress Cataloging-in-Publication Data

Phillips, Larissa.
Cochise: Apache chief / by Larissa Phillips.
 p. cm. — (Primary sources of famous people in American history)
Summary: A biography of this Chiricahua chief who led his people in battle for many years, trying to preserve their independence.
Includes bibliographical references and index.
ISBN 0-8239-4105-1 (lib. bdg.: alk. paper)
ISBN 0-8239-4177-9 (pbk.: alk. paper)
6-pack ISBN 0-8239-4304-6
1. Cochise, Apache chief, d. 1874. 2. Chiricahua Indians—Kings and rulers—Biography.
3. Chiricahua Indians—Wars. 4. Chiricahua Indians—Government relations. 5. Apache Indians—Wars, 1872–1873. [1. Cochise, Apache chief, d. 1874. 2. Chiricahua Indians—Biography. 3. Apache Indians—Biography. 4. Indians of North America—New Mexico—Biography. 5. Kings, queens, rulers, etc.]
I. Title. II. Series.
E99.A6C5746 2004
979.004'972—dc21

                                                                                  2003005182

Manufactured in the United States of America

Photo credits: cover illustration by Peggy Flanders; pp. 5, 6, 12, 13, 16, 17, 19 (top), 24 Western History Collection, University of Oklahoma; pp. 7 (X-32936), 10 (L-287), 20 (X-33736), 26 (X-32866), 27 (X-33462) Denver Public Library, Western History Collection; p. 8 courtesy of the Louisiana Old State Capitol Center for Political and Governmental History and the Randy Haynie Family Collection; p. 9 © The Art Archive/National Palace Mexico City/Dagli Orti; p. 11 © Underwood Photo Archives/SuperStock, Inc.; p. 14 Kansas State Historical Society; pp. 15, 25 National Archives and Records Administration; p. 19 (bottom) © Corbis; pp. 21, 23 (left), 28 © Hulton/Archive/Getty Images; p. 23 (right) Huntington Library, San Marino, CA; p. 29 © The Art Archive/National Archives, Washington, DC.

Designer: Thomas Forget; Editor: Joann Jovinelly; Photo Researcher: Rebecca Anguin-Cohen

CONTENTS

1 A BORN LEADER

Historians believe that Cochise was born in 1812, in what is now the state of Arizona. He was a member of the Apache Nation of Native Americans. Cochise had been raised to be a warrior. For the Apache, fighting was a way of life.

TRIBES OF THE APACHE NATION

The Apache Nation is actually a grouping of six culturally related Native American tribes that originated in the Southwest. Cochise was a member of the Chiricahua tribe. The other five tribes were known as the Mescalero, the Mimbreno, the Lipan, the Jicarilla, and the Kiowa. The word "Apache" may have come from the Zuni word for enemy.

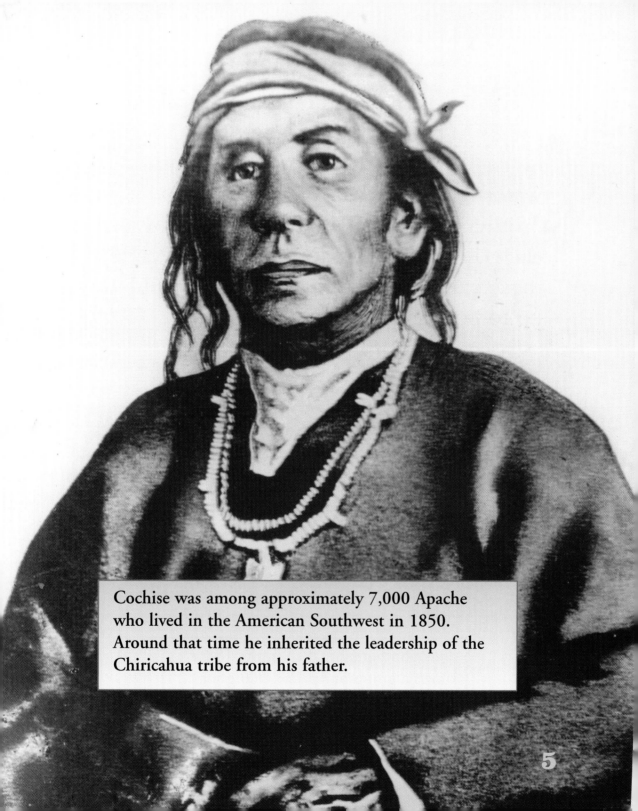

Cochise was among approximately 7,000 Apache who lived in the American Southwest in 1850. Around that time he inherited the leadership of the Chiricahua tribe from his father.

Like his three brothers, Cochise played games to build discipline. In one such game, he had to run for hours with a mouthful of water without swallowing it. He and his brothers also practiced shooting arrows at each other for accuracy. Cochise excelled at these games. It was clear that he would grow up to be a great fighter.

This photograph, taken in the 1880s, shows a group of Apache youngsters playing a game in San Carlos, Arizona.

Cochise's wife Toos-day-zay is pictured in this studio portrait taken between 1884 and 1885.

2 LOSING GROUND

Cochise's tribe was called the Chiricahua. They were part of the Apache Nation. They lived in what is now Arizona and New Mexico. For almost 300 years, his people had battled the Spanish and Mexicans from the south. The Spaniards were mostly interested in mining gold and gaining wealth.

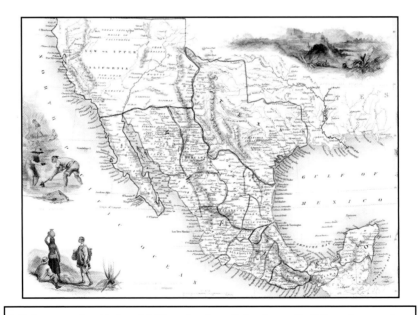

This map by John Tallis depicts Mexico, California, and Texas in 1851. At the time, populations of Indians in these areas were equal to whites.

This painting by Diego Rivera depicts fighting during the Mexican-American War (1846–1848). The conflict lasted two years and killed thousands of people on both sides.

The Apache did not know their most powerful enemy was about to come. For years the American settlers and miners had been moving westward, building towns, farms, and mining camps. The settlers didn't care that they were mining land occupied by Native Americans.

Nineteenth-century Colorado is shown in this photograph of a mining settlement. This is an example of how harvesting natural resources helped establish the Southwest during the period of westward expansion.

Many men such as this one traveled west to become miners, especially after California's 1848 gold rush. In many cases, people were offered plots of land from the federal government in exchange for future mining profits.

The American settlers pushed farther and farther into Apache territory. They used guns, liquor, and sometimes even diseased blankets to kill and weaken the Native Americans. Naturally, the Apache fought back. They called their new enemies the "White Eyes."

The Apache dwelling shown in this photograph is the skeleton of a traditional wickiup, a circular or oval structure of arched poles that is covered with brush or preserved animal hides.

These photographs of Apache women sitting by their wickiups were taken around 1880. Apache women often gathered wild edible plants and helped harvest crops such as corn, beans, and squash.

3   KIDNAPPED!

In February of 1861, a white man reported that the Apache had raided his cattle ranch. He claimed that the Native Americans had kidnapped his son. A young U.S. lieutenant named George N. Bascom requested a meeting with Cochise to solve the matter. Cochise brought members of his family to the meeting in order to show his trust.

This illustration, drawn in 1867, shows how cattle were driven across the western plains during the early years of the United States.

Lieutenant George N. Bascom, shown in this photograph, did not believe Cochise's claim that another Apache tribe was responsible for the kidnapping. Cochise's story was later proven accurate.

Cochise denied the charge, but Bascom arrested him, anyway. Cochise quickly cut his way out of the tent. While running to safety, one of Cochise's tribesmen was killed. Then, the Americans killed Cochise's brother and two of his relatives. After this, the conflict intensified. Both the Americans and the Native Americans called for vengeance in the Apache Wars.

Cochise taught his family to fight for their tribal lands. Cochise's son Naiche (also spelled Na-chise or Naatchez), pictured on the far left, continued this fight after his father's death in 1874.

Naiche, seen in this photograph with a gun, is standing beside his wife, Ha-o-zinne. Native Americans realized that in order to protect their territories, they needed firearms.

17

4 THE APACHE WARS

The United States had a powerful army outfitted with many guns. But the Apache were a fearsome enemy. Cochise was a brilliant leader. He set up complicated ambushes. He was filled with rage for the deaths of his people and the loss of their land.

THE INDIAN WARS

The Indian Wars and those specifically related to the Apache tribes (known as the Apache Wars) were fought between 1865 and 1890. These conflicts occurred between Europeans and their descendants and the Native Americans living in lands that later became the United States.

Native Americans acquired firearms through trade with whites, but their increased use of manufactured goods made them less independent. Soon it became even easier for them to be forced from tribal lands.

The conflict continued for years. Thousands of Apache and Americans were killed. The United States made an offer to move the Apache people to a reservation in New Mexico if they would stop the killing. Cochise refused. He thought the life of a coyote, always running but free, was better than the life of a dog, begging for scraps.

By the mid-nineteenth century, Americans were pushing farther west into lands that had been originally settled by Native American tribes, including the Apache, seen in this illustration defending their territory.

These photographs visibly show the changes that the Apache tribes experienced after just four months in a reservation school. Whites believed that Native Americans needed to be more "civilized."

In those days, the lives of U.S. Pony Express mail carriers were at great risk. The Apache often killed them. A mail carrier named Thomas Jeffords decided to speak to Cochise. He walked alone into the Apache camp. Cochise was impressed with his bravery. After several days of talking, Cochise agreed to let the mail carriers pass unharmed.

THE PONY EXPRESS

The Pony Express was a U.S. mail system that was operated by a team of expert riders between 1860 and 1861. Men rode horseback on stretches of 75 to 100 miles through the present-day states of Kansas, Nebraska, Colorado, Wyoming, Utah, Nevada, and California.

Thomas Jeffords, a U.S. Army scout and messenger, was among the only American white men Cochise trusted. Jeffords earned Cochise's respect because of his bravery.

After this, the army asked Jeffords to help end the Apache Wars. In 1872, Jeffords convinced Cochise to meet with a tough, one-armed general named Oliver O. Howard. General Howard offered Cochise and his people a distant plot of land where the water was polluted and the winters were cold.

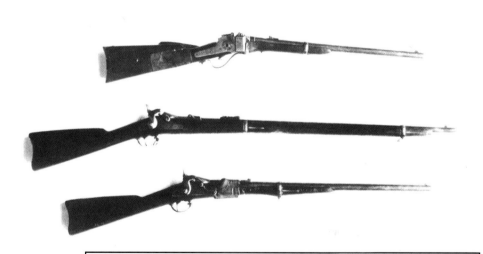

Members of Native American tribes once owned the firearms in this photograph. The Native Americans first gained the use of firearms from the Spanish, whom they fought years earlier.

Pictured in this photograph is one-armed General Oliver O. Howard, famous for his fighting in the U.S. Civil War but also for his campaigns against Native Americans.

25

5 THE SURRENDER

By 1872, Cochise and his people were hungry and tired. Thousands of Native American children had been orphaned. Great warriors had been killed. Cochise wanted to settle. He requested a new reservation be established in Apache Pass in the Chiricahua Mountains. General Howard agreed. The Apache Wars were over.

This photograph shows a group of Apache who were kept as prisoners between 1884 and 1885 at Fort Bowie, in what is now present-day Arizona.

The Native American men pictured in this photograph are posing with a white man near Fort Apache, Arizona, in 1883.

Cochise died on the reservation two years later. After his death, the reservation dissolved. By then the Apache people had either left or were relocated. Although Cochise won many battles against the White Eyes, he lost the war. He is remembered and respected as a brilliant leader and a great Apache hero.

This rock formation in Arizona is known as Cochise's Head. Its natural contours remind people of Cochise's profile.

This young Native American princess, seen here in traditional dress, is the granddaughter of Cochise, the Apache chief of the Chiricahua tribe.

TIMELINE

1812—Year in which historians believe Cochise was born in present-day Arizona.

1846-1848—Mexican-American War.

1861—Cochise is taken prisoner but is able to cut his way out of a tent and escape.

1865-1890—Indian Wars period.

1863—Cochise becomes a war chief.

1867—Thomas Jeffords meets with and befriends Cochise.

1872—Cochise escapes rather than allow his people to be moved to a New Mexico reservation; The Apache move to a reservation covering most of southeast Arizona.

June 8, 1874—Cochise dies at the reservation in Arizona.

GLOSSARY

ambush (AM-bush) To lie in wait and then launch a surprise attack.

Apache Nation (uh-PACH-ee NAY-shun) The huge group of tribes in the southwestern area of the United States.

raid (RAYD) A surprise attack, sometimes through a village to steal horses or cattle.

reservation (REH-zer-VAY-shun) An area of land set aside by the government for a special purpose.

tribe (TRYB) A group of families who are closely related.

vengeance (VEN-jents) To punish as an act of revenge.

WEB SITES

Due to the changing nature of Internet links, the Rosen Publishing Group, Inc., has developed an online list of Web sites related to the subject of this book. This site is updated regularly. Please use this link to access the list:

http://www.rosenlinks.com/fpah/coch

PRIMARY SOURCE IMAGE LIST

Pages 5–6: These photographs are part of the Noah H. Rose collection of images from the University of Oklahoma in Norman, OK.

Page 7: Cochise's wife Toos-day-zay is pictured in this photograph that is part of the collection of the Denver Public Library and Historical Society in Denver, Colorado.

Page 8: An 1851 map of Mexico, California, and Texas drawn by John Tallis is housed in the private collection of Randy Haynie.

Page 10: Central City, Colorado, seen in this 1899 photograph taken by Harry H. Lake, is now part of the collection of the Denver Public Library and Historical Society in Denver, Colorado.

Page 11: This photograph of a miner was taken in the 1800s.

Pages 12–13: These photographs are part of the Noah H. Rose collection of images from the University of Oklahoma in Norman, OK.

Page 15: This image of George N. Bascom is a part of the collection of the National Archives in Washington, DC.

Pages 16–19: These photographs are part of the Noah H. Rose collection of images from the University of Oklahoma in Norman, OK.

Page 19: Timothy H. O'Sullivan took this photograph of Apache Indians ready for battle in 1873.

Page 21: John N. Choate took these photographs of Native American children in 1886.

Page 23 (left): Created around 1861, this is an original advertising poster for the Pony Express U.S. mail service.

Page 23 (right): Thomas Jeffords, a friend of Cochise and Pony Express rider, is seen in this photograph that is now a part of the collection of the Huntington Library in San Marino, California.

Page 24: This photograph of firearms belonging to several Native Americans is a part of the collection of W. S. Campbell.

Page 25: Civil War General Oliver O. Howard is pictured in this photograph that is now part of the collection of the National Archives in Washington, DC.

Page 26: The Native American prisoners seen in this 1884 photograph, taken in Fort Bowie, Arizona, is now part of the collection of prints at the Denver Public Library and Historical Society in Denver, CO.

Page 27: Ben Wittick took this photograph of Native American men in Fort Apache, Arizona, now a part of the collection of prints at the Denver Public Library and Historical Society in Denver, Colorado.

Page 29: Cochise's granddaughter, seen in this historic studio photograph, is a part of the collection of the National Archives in Washington, DC.

INDEX

ABOUT THE AUTHOR

Larissa Phillips is a freelance writer who lives in Brooklyn, New York.